Simple Machines

Screws

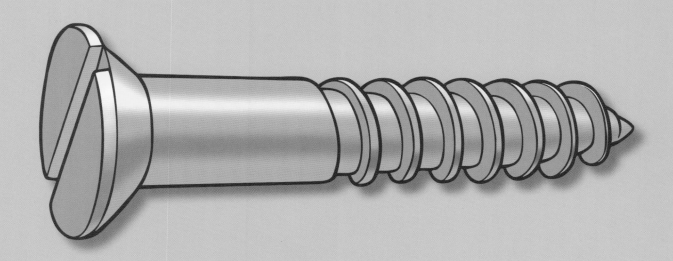

Chris Oxlade

A⁺

Smart Apple Media

Published by Smart Apple Media
2140 Howard Drive West
North Mankato, MN 56003

Designed by Helen James
Edited by Mary-Jane Wilkins
Artwork by Bill Donohoe

Photo credits
page 5 photo provided by permission from scienceshareware.com; 6 Lester Lefkowitz/
Corbis; 9 Krista Kennell/Zuma/Corbis; 11 Andrew Lambert Photography/Science Photo
Library; 12 Layne Kennedy/Corbis; 14 David Gallant/Corbis; 16 Jennie Woodcock;
Reflections Photolibrary/Corbis; 19 Alan Towse; Ecoscene/Corbis; 20 Deere & Company;
22 Underwood & Underwood/Corbis; 23 Time Life Pictures/Getty Images; 28 Gehl
Company/Corbis; 29 Krista Kennell/Zuma/Corbis

Printed in China

Library of Congress Cataloging-in-Publication Data

Oxlade, Chris.
Screws / by Chris Oxlade.
p. cm. — (Simple machines)
Includes index.
ISBN 978-1-59920-085-9
1. Screws—Juvenile literature. 2. Simple machines—Juvenile literature. [1. Screws.] I. Title.

TJ1338.O89 2007
621.8'82—dc22   2007004880

First Edition

9 8 7 6 5 4 3 2 1

Contents

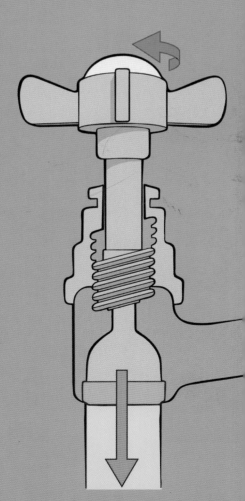

What is a simple machine?

A simple machine is something that helps you do a job. We use simple machines to help us every day. Here are some simple machines you might have at home.

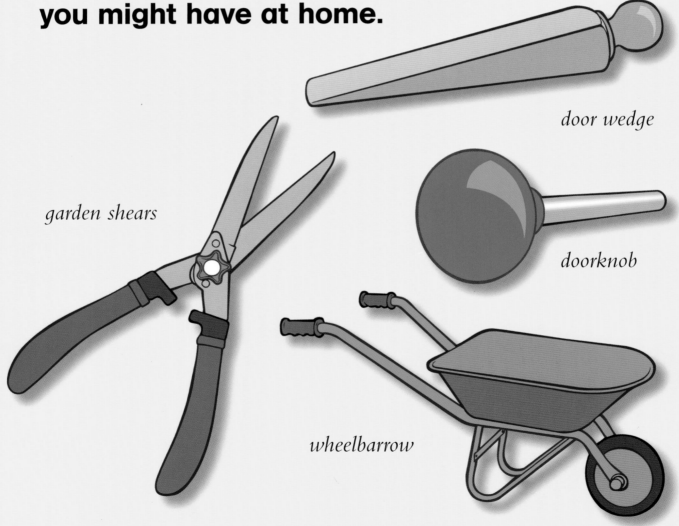

door wedge

garden shears

doorknob

wheelbarrow

This book is about simple machines called screws. A bolt is a type of screw. We use bolts to connect things. Corkscrews, construction screws, and drill bits are screws, too.

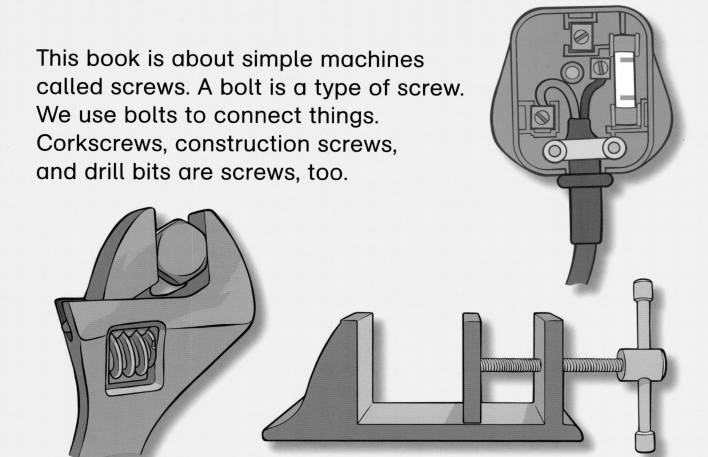

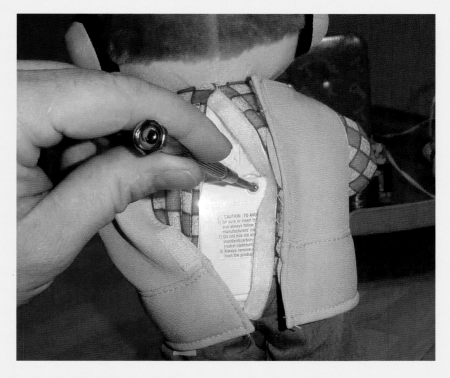

Turning a screw attaches the battery cover to this toy.

Pushes and pulls

You turn a screw to make it work. To turn it, you push and pull on it. When you push and pull, the screw also makes a push or pull. Scientists call all pushes and pulls "forces."

Pushing on the wrench turns the bolt. The bolt pulls on the nut.

On paper, arrows show pushes and pulls. The arrow points in the direction of the pushing or pulling force. A longer arrow means a bigger push or pull.

Red arrows show pushes and pulls.

Blue arrows show movement.

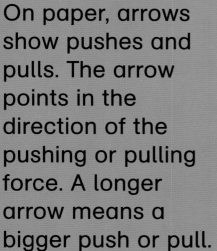

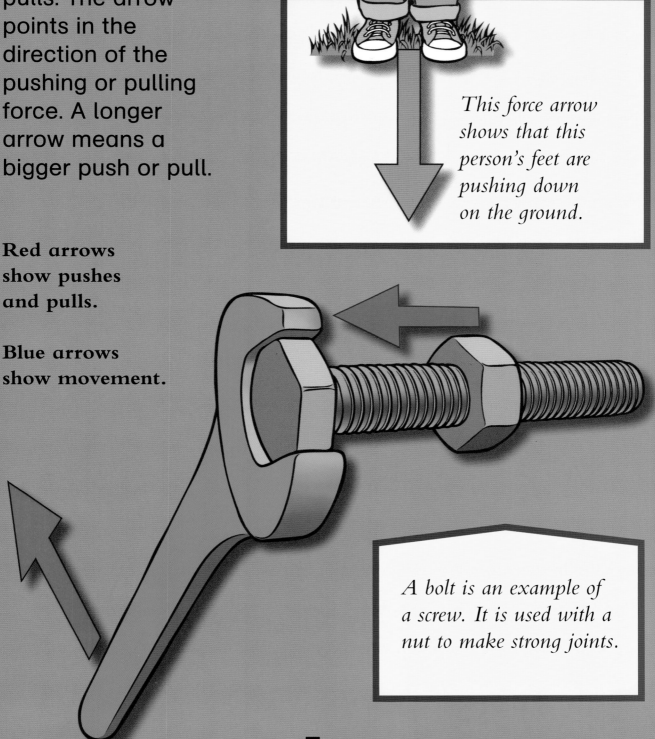

This force arrow shows that this person's feet are pushing down on the ground.

A bolt is an example of a screw. It is used with a nut to make strong joints.

How a screw works

A screw is a simple machine. It is a rod with a spiral around the outside. The spiral is called a screw thread. A screw only works when the thread pushes against something.

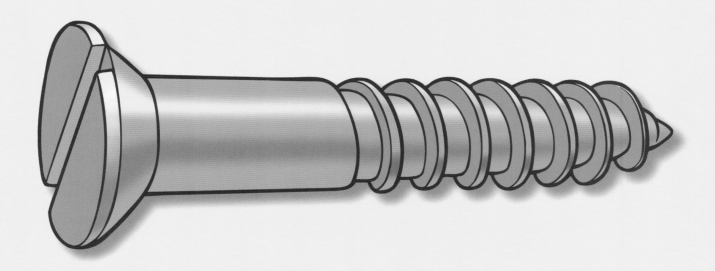

This is a simple screw. The thread goes around and around the outside of the screw.

When a screw is turned, the thread pushes or pulls the material the screw is pressing against. This makes the screw move into the material.

Sometimes a turning screw, such as a drill bit, moves the material instead. A small push or pull on the screw makes a large push or pull on the material.

Gently turning a bottle top makes it grip the bottle tightly.

Lifting with screws

We use screws to help lift heavy things. A screw jack is a machine that lifts and supports heavy objects. Turning the screw jack makes the screw rise out of the base.

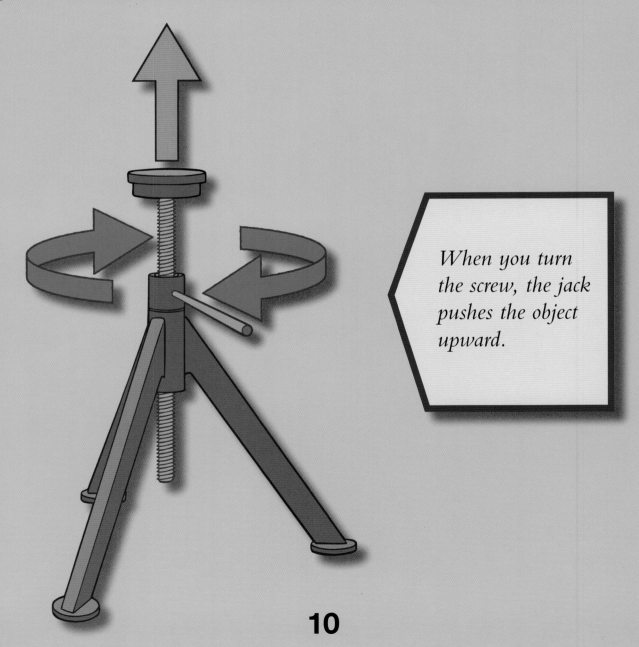

When you turn the screw, the jack pushes the object upward.

A scissor jack helps lift a car so the tire can be changed.

The screw pulls the sides of the scissor jack together. This pushes the top of the jack upward.

Pushing and pulling makes the handle turn. This pushes the car up.

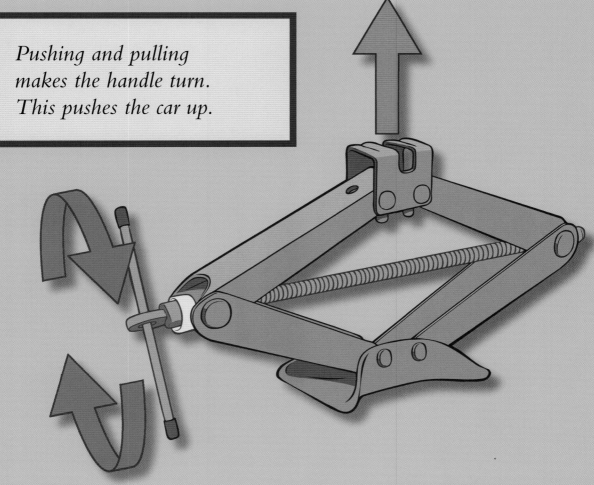

Gripping with screws

We use screws to grip things tightly. We use a C-clamp for holding objects together while we glue them. A small bar turns the screw.

C-clamps press pieces of wood together to make a birch-bark canoe.

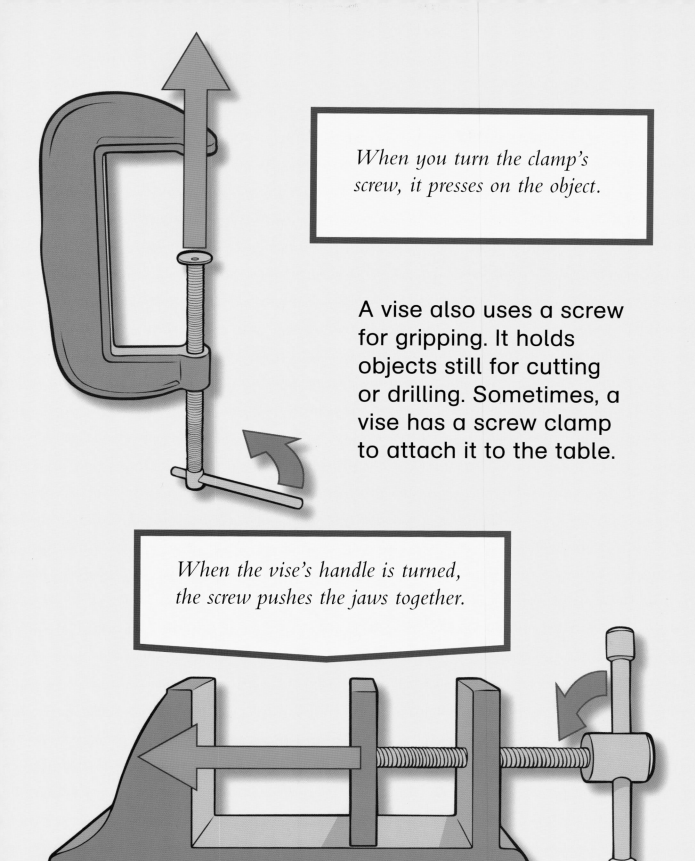

When you turn the clamp's screw, it presses on the object.

A vise also uses a screw for gripping. It holds objects still for cutting or drilling. Sometimes, a vise has a screw clamp to attach it to the table.

When the vise's handle is turned, the screw pushes the jaws together.

Squeezing with screws

We use screws to squeeze things. A cider press squeezes the juice from apples.

The cider press has a large screw in the center. Turning the handles moves a pad down the screw, pressing it down on the apples.

A pull on the handles makes a larger push, which crushes the apples.

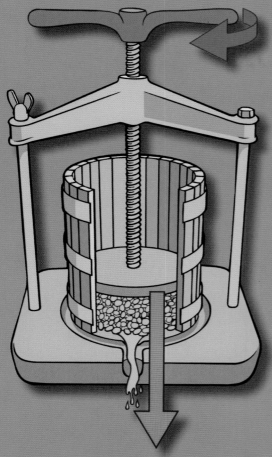

When the cider press handles are pulled, the pad presses on the apples.

There is a rubber washer inside a water faucet that will keep water from flowing out. Turning the faucet handle turns a screw. This screw squeezes the washer against the end of the water pipe, turning off the water.

When the faucet handle is pushed, the screw pushes down on the rubber washer.

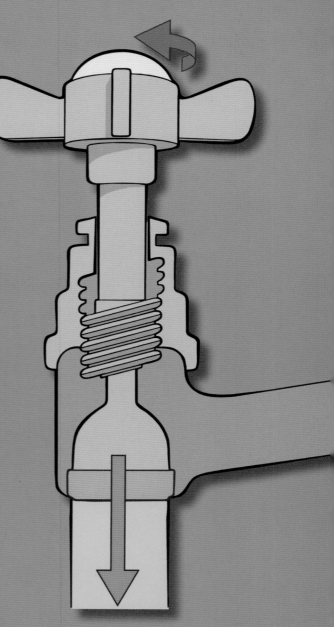

Connecting with screws

We use screws to connect things. A screw is a piece of metal with a sharp screw thread and a pointed end. It is used to connect pieces of wood, plastic, or metal.

Can you see the bolts that help hold this play set together?

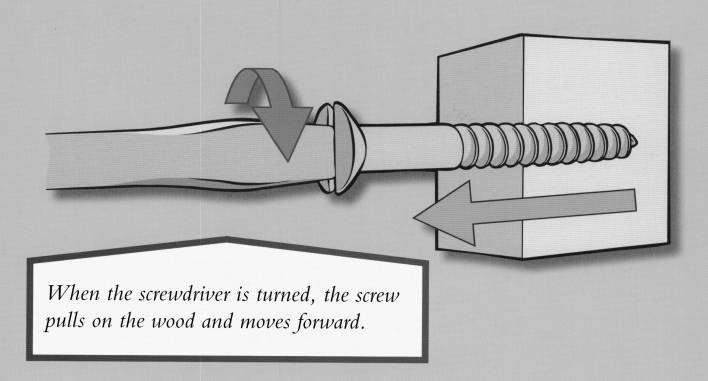

When the screwdriver is turned, the screw pulls on the wood and moves forward.

A nut and bolt are used to connect pieces of material. The screw threads on the nut and bolt fit together. When the bolt is turned, it pulls on the nut.

When the bolt turns, it pulls on the nut.

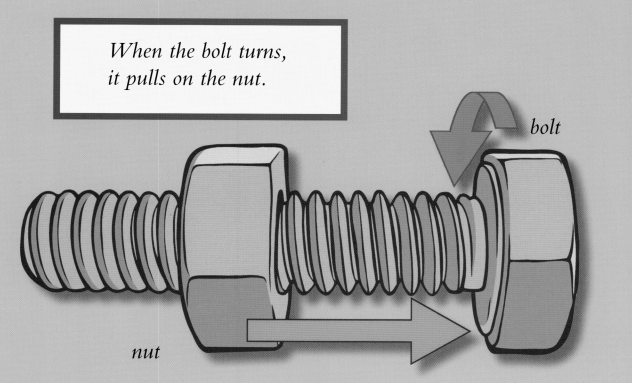

bolt

nut

Moving with screws

We use screws to move materials from place to place. A drill bit for drilling wood and brick has a screw thread.

The cutting blades of the drill break off small bits of material. As the drill bit turns, the screw thread moves waste materials out of the hole.

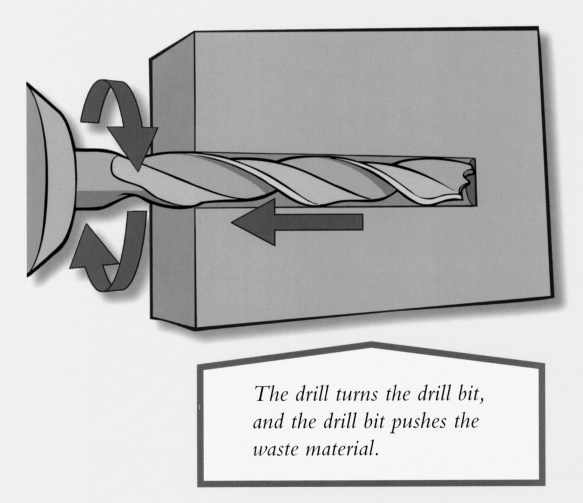

The drill turns the drill bit, and the drill bit pushes the waste material.

A machine called a screw conveyor moves materials in factories. Inside the conveyor is a screw with a wide thread. As the screw turns, material is caught by the thread and pushed along.

This screw conveyor is moving plastics through a recycling plant. Can you see the screw thread?

A motor turns the screw. The screw pushes the material along the conveyor.

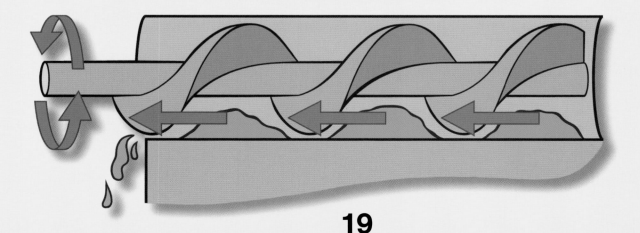

Screws in machines

Complicated machines often use screws to work.

A combine harvester cuts down crops and separates the grain from the stalks. A screw at the front of the machine collects the crop.

The screw moves the cut crop sideways.

An adjustable wrench can be used on bolts of any size. It has a screw that moves the jaws together to grip the nut.

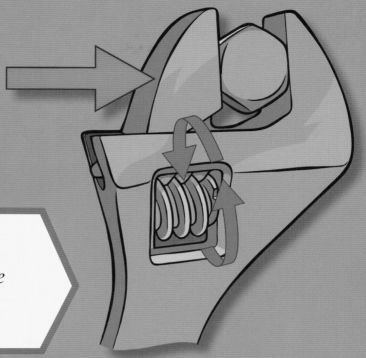

A wrench's jaws can be adjusted with one finger. The wrench grips the nut tightly.

This motor has a worm gear. A worm gear is a special type of gear that uses a screw. This screw makes the gear turn slowly.

When the screw turns quickly, the wheel turns slowly.

21

Screws in the past

People have been using screws for thousands of years.

The printing press was invented more than 500 years ago. To print pages for a book, the large wooden screw presses ink-covered, metal letters onto paper.

Can you see the giant screw that works this press?

Romans watching an Archimedean screw lifting water.

This is an Archimedean screw. It was invented thousands of years ago to bring water from rivers to the fields for crops.

The screw conveyor on page 19 is a modern version of this simple machine.

Fun with screws

The activities on the next four pages will help you understand how screws work.

A MODEL SCREW JACK

You will need:
- a large nut and bolt (you could use a nut and bolt from a model construction kit)
- an old CD
- modeling clay or tape

| 1 | Put the nut over the hole in the middle of the CD. |

2 Attach the nut to the CD with modeling clay or tape.

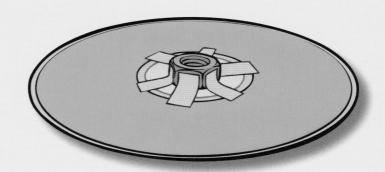

3 Put the CD flat on a table with the nut underneath.

4 Screw the bolt slowly into the nut while you hold the CD.

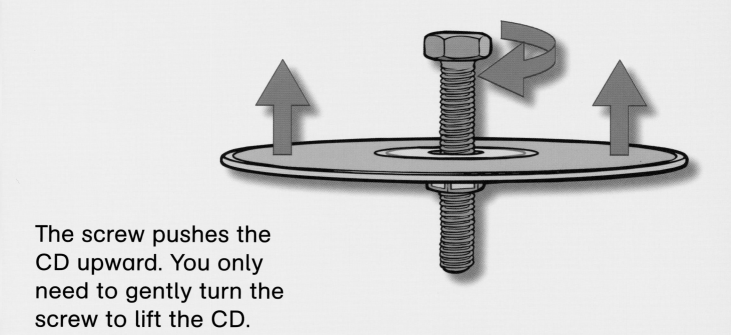

The screw pushes the CD upward. You only need to gently turn the screw to lift the CD.

A screw conveyor

You will need:
- a pencil
- a piece of thin rope about 16 inches (40 cm) long
- tape
- a note card, six inches by three inches (15 x 8 cm)
- dried beans or peas

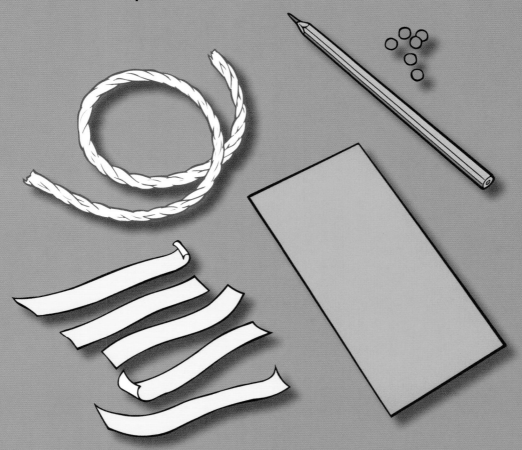

1 Tape one end of the rope to one end of the pencil.

2 Wrap the rope tightly around the pencil.
Spread the rope spirals along the pencil.
Tape the rope to the other end of the pencil.

3 Wrap the note card around the
pencil and rope to make a tube.

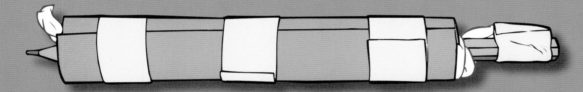

4

Drop some of the dried
beans or peas into the
card tube.

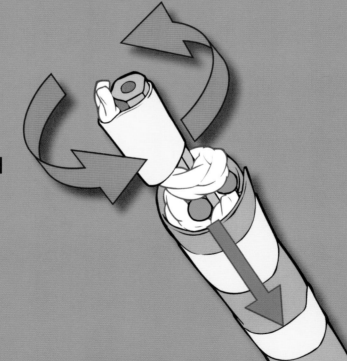

When you turn the pencil, the rope screw
will move the beans or peas along the tube.

Find the screws

Can you find all the screws on these pages? Try to figure out what each screw does.

This screw moves material upward. What is the material?

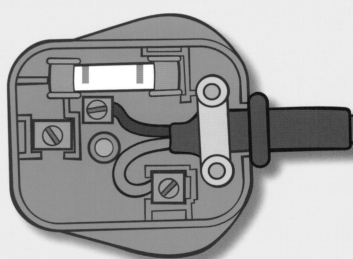

Can you see
the screw here?
What does it do?

These screws are
inside an electric plug.
What do they grip?

Answers are on page 32.

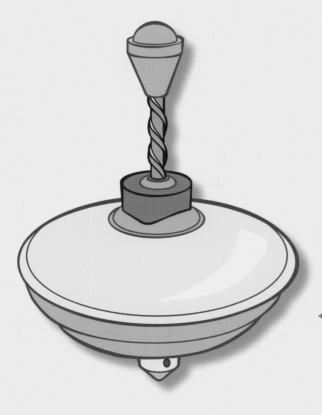

Where is the screw
thread in this toy?

Words to remember

Archimedean screw
A tube with a screw inside that lifts water uphill when it is turned.

C-clamp
A clamp shaped like a capital letter C that uses a screw to hold two pieces of material together.

drill bit
A rod with a sharp blade at one end and a screw thread along the outside that is turned to drill holes.

forces
Pushes or pulls.

screw conveyor
A machine that uses a wide screw thread to move loose or liquid materials from place to place.

screw jack

A machine that uses a screw to lift
heavy objects upward.

screw thread

The spiral ridge around a bolt or screw.

vise

A machine that is used to grip objects tightly while
they are cut or drilled. A vise is usually attached to a
bench or table.

worm gear

A screw and a gear wheel that work together.
When the screw turns quickly, the wheel turns slowly.

wrench

A lever used to turn a nut or bolt.
An adjustable wrench can turn
nuts and bolts of various sizes.

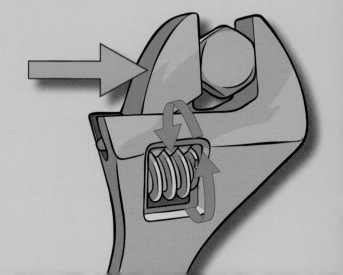

Index

Answers to pages 28–29

The screw is called an auger. It moves dirt.

This is a corkscrew. It pulls a cork out of a bottle.

You can see the ends of three screws. They grip wires.

The screw is near the top. It makes the top spin when you push down.